A Liturgy for Humanists

A Liturgy for Humanists

Turning Our Beliefs Into Actions

Robert W. Christie

A Liturgy for Humanists: Turning Our Beliefs Into Actions

Robert W. Christie

copyright © 2014 by Robert W. Christie, all rights reserved

published 2014 by Martin Meadow Press

ISBN: 978-0-9913315-4-3

all images except those on pages 44 and 64 by Robert W. Christie

5

A Liturgy for Humanists

**Beliefs and Meditations
for**
Humanists…
Agnostics…
Atheists…
Christians…
Unitarians…
Quakers…
Muslims…
Jews…
**and for others who might consider themselves
spiritual…but not religious.**

An excursion into a contemporary liturgy with a codification of beliefs and meditations for those open-minded, intellectually humanistic individuals seeking an informed corporate religious service.

"The priest departs, the divine literatus comes."
Walt Whitman

Contents

The Humanist's Task

The secular questioning mind
is the greatest challenge
to established dogmatic religious beliefs.
The Humanist's task
is to hammer away at the
rock of dogmatic religious traditons
and to use the flying chips
to build, chip by chip, a new
citadel of credible religious beliefs.

Religion and Morality

Religion and morality are
indispensable supports for political prosperity.
Let us with caution indulge the supposition
that morality can be maintained without religion.
…reason and experience both forbid us
to expect that national morality can prevail
in exclusion of religious principle.

George Washington

A Template for a Humanist's Liturgy

Do Humanists Need a Liturgy?
Hymn: "Ode to Joy" *Ludwig von Beethoven*
Creation's Trinity and Definitions
Reassurances
Beliefs and Meditations
Deep Questions and Deep Responses
Responsibility: *Saint Teresa of Avila*
Seeking God: *Judah Ha-Levi*
Brotherhood: *Muhammad*
A Spiritual Life's Foundations: *Nelson Mandela*
Love: *Jesus of Nazareth*
War and Peace: *Edward O. Wilson*
Hymn: "Finlandia: This Is My Song" *Jean Sibelius*
An Humanist's Religious Responsibility
The Peace
Benediction

14

Do Humanists Need a Liturgy?

Yes.
Humanism has quietly emerged as a secular religion based on values.

Humanism includes belief in values to which one ascribes supreme
importance, without acknowledging a supreme controlling deity.
Yet the absence of a liturgy based on humanistic values leaves many with a
yearning for a format in which to share religious experiences and values
based on reality and tenable and substantiated truths, rather than
worship based on sacred texts, faith, prayer, and an enigmatic deity.
The meditations in this liturgy offer all persons a format in which to
share with others their beliefs, behaviors, and their charitable options.
It recognizes the realities in their lives, their responsibilities in the world
in which they live, and transfers from a deity to themselves the
responsibility for their own behavior during a brief existence on Earth.

Ode to Joy
Ludwig von Beethoven

Joyful, joyful, we adore thee, God of glory, Lord of love;
Hearts unfold like flowers before thee, Praising thee, their sun above.
Melt the clouds of sin and sadness; Drive the dark of doubt away.
Giver of immortal gladness, Fill us with the light of day.

Mortals, join the mighty chorus, Which the morning stars began.
Father love is reigning o'er us; Brother love binds man to man.
Ever singing, march we onward, Victors in the midst of strife.
Joyful music lifts us sunward, In the triumph song of life.

Reassurances

These meditations are meant to be neither
a substitute for nor a replacement of traditional forms of worship,
whose rituals, prayers, practices and creeds
for many bring a sufficient and fulfilling measure
of spiritual satisfaction and inner peace.
Their purpose is rather to offer an opportunity
for those disaffected young and old of whatever belief or unbelief
to meditate in a liturgical format, using occasionally
a visual centering focus that allows the meditator
to avoid the distractions of
arcane scriptural myths,
prophecies, revelations, dogmas and liturgical rituals
that are not longer believable within our present understanding.
The revelations of science, Francis Bacon's "new religion,"
have helped guide Humanists to arrive at
more reasonable, rational and verifiable truths and beliefs.

Beliefs and Definitions
Creation's Trinity

Understanding the definitions of the words we use commonly in worship is imperative when discussing matters of religion and faith, agape and lust, life and death. It is too easy to assume that everyone knows what is being referred to theologically or liturgically when we use terms such as God, ethics, morality, love, faith or soul in our liturgies,
but that is surely questionable.
We would do well by putting our traditional theological constructions aside, and accept the basic and immutable trinity in nature, controlling all life:

Procreation • Competition • Selection

Therefore, in the liturgical meditations following, perhaps you will find helpful several fairly rigorous paraphrased expositions from the *New Oxford American Dictionary* of how the words we frequently bandy about—too often thoughtlessly in our rote religious recitations—have been objectively defined by linguists, rather than by theologians, preachers, professional clergy, or as found within purportedly sacred writings or liturgical texts.

Agape: Christian love, esp. as distinct from erotic love.

Agnosticism: Belief that nothing is known or can be known of the existence of nature of God or of anything beyond material phenomena; neither faith in, nor disbelief in "God".

Atheism: Disbelief in the existence of God or gods.

Ethics: A body of moral principles, values, or right conduct governing or distinctive of a particular culture or group; a complex of moral precepts or rules of conduct.

Faith: Confidence or trust in a person or thing; belief that is not based on proof, and therefore susceptible to skepticism or disbelief.

God: Commonly, an anthropomorphic controlling being worthy of worship and supplication, existing elsewhere in the cosmos; in Christianity and other monotheistic religions, the creator and ruler of the universe and source of all moral auhtority; the supreme being; in non-monotheistic religions, a superhuman being or spirit worshiped as having power over nature or human fortunes.

Holy Spirit: God as spiritually active in the world; in Christianity, the third person of the Trinity. The term "spirituality" is enigmatic, i.e., difficult to define.

Humanism: Belief that nothing is known or can be known of the existence or nature of God or of anything beyond material phenomena; neither faith in/nor disbelief in a god, and stressing the potential value and goodness of humans seeking rational ways to solve human problems.　　21

Liturgy: A form according to which public Christian worship is conducted.

Morals: The rules of ethical conduct by which a socieity exhorts its members to behavior consistent with order, security, and growth, and which change as societies progress from ages of hunting-gathering, agriculture, and industry, to the age of science and communication, with its consequent emancipation from theological prophecies, terrors, and sins, desinged to control behavior through assignment of personal guilt and need for its expiation by prayer, granted by priesthoods.

Soul: The principle of life, feeling, thought and action guiding humans, regarded as a distinct entity and separable in its existence from the physical body; an incorporation of "God" (see prior definition on previous page) within the human mind, and often, paradoxically, an organ incorporated in the human body.

Spirit: The nonphysical part of a person that is the seat of emotion and character; a person's true self, capable of surviving physical death or separation.

Visual Images for Meditation

The images presented
are to provide a focus for
the concerns to be meditated upon
before taking on the duties,
responsibilities, and cares
of the day before you…

...which may often seem overwhelming.

Meditation

Great Issues

Meditations
for individual concentration…
on one, a few, many, or all
of those Great Issues and Questions
included here…or your own
may vary in length of time devoted to them.

In groups or gatherings,
a consensus may determine a time or focus
for these, or other meditations.

Thus meditate quietly,
and respond to the spirit within you speaking…

Baffin Island, Nunavut, Canada

about
our insignificance
within a cosmos
indifferent to the transient existence
of our species…

Stoa of Attalos, Athens, Greece

about
our
anthropocentric
arrogance and hubris…
and our unwillingness to admit
that there are deep realities forever
beyond human comprehension…

Mt. Hood, Cascade Range, Oregon

about
Earth's majesty…
and its paper-thin biosphere's fragility…

Persisting life on Earth: Great black-backed gull chicks

about
the powers of Nature…
asteroid impacts…
earthquakes…
tsunamis…
volcanic eruptions…
fires…
floods…
droughts…
tornadoes…
hurricanes…
…and the vulnerability of all life on Earth

Grieving Believers

about
grief…
and those amongst us grieving,
for whatever reason…

Alone

about
loneliness,
at any age…

about
our thoughtless disregard
of the
Ten Commandments
as a moral guide…
in all monotheistic religions…
or for atheists…

The Ten Commandments

The rules of conduct allegedly given by God to Moses on Mount Sinai,
according to Exodus 20:1–17; regarded currently as a moral guide.

I. Have no other gods.

II. Do not make or worship idols.

III. Do not take the name of the Lord in vain.

IV. Keep the Sabbath holy.

V. Honor one's father and mother.

VI. Do not kill.

VII. Do not commit adultery.

VIII. Do not steal.

IX. Do not give false evidence.

X. Do not covet another's property or wife.

Fallen Leaves
Holocaust Museum, Berlin, Germany

about
genocide…

Unintentional martyrs:
American Cemetery, Normandy, France

about
warfare
and
man's inhumanity to man…

Cologne, Germany, 1945

about
the greatest of human follies…
war,
and its antecedents,
fear, greed, revenge, national pride,
and narrow-minded religious fervor
based on unfounded or unproven beliefs,
ignorance, and gullibility,
invariably leading to
unanticipated consequences…

Holy Cross Monastery
West Park, New York

about
reverence for life
ecological perservation
environmental sustainability
and social justice
as religious issues…

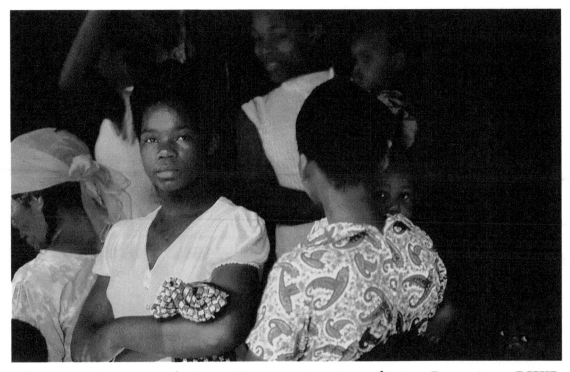

Burgeoning population: Immunization clinic, Jamaica, BWI

about
the overwhelming primary
problem before us…
Earth's unsustainable human species
overpopulation
increasing by 16,000 newborn
every hour…

about
the inevitable
Malthusian consequences of
human overpopulation…
environmental destruction…
starvation…
epidemic disease…
genocide…
war…

Deep Questions and Responses

The First Deep Question

*Who am I
and
what can I do?*

Who am I?… what can I do?

The Next Deep Question

Where was I before a moment of
parental procreational passion
brought me from not being
into existing…?
Where will I be when I am once again
transformed by death from existing
into disappearing forever…?

What worthwhile thing can I do *now* in the world
while I live in this brief interval
between never having existed
and disappearing forever…?

Rural village, Netherlands

Responses to Deep Questions

Communication

A Monastic Theologian's Deep Questions Response
Where Responsibility Lies

God has no body but ours,
no hands but ours,
no feet but ours.
Ours are the eyes through which
God's compassion
must look out on the world.
Ours are the hands
which God arouses now.
Ours are the feet
with which to go about
doing good.
                    St. Teresa of Avila

A Rabbi's Deep Thoughts Response:
Seeking and Finding God

Lord, where shall I find thee?
High and hidden is thy place;
And where shall I not find thee?
The world is full of thy glory.
I have sought thy nearness,
With all my heart I called thee,
And going out to meet thee,
I found thee coming toward me.

Judah Ha-Levi

A Religion's Founder's Deep Thoughts Response
Brotherhood

"Know that every believer is a believer's brother,
and all believers are brethren.
No one is to be forced to convert,
and Christians and Jews especially are to be respected.
Those who embrace Islam of their own accord,
they are among the faithful,
with the same privileges and obligations,
but if they hold fast to their tradition,
they are not to be seduced from it."
Muhammad
Quran

60

A Nobel Laureate's Deep Thoughts Response
A Spiritual Life's Foundations

Honesty, sincerity, simplicity,
humility, pure generosity,
absence of vanity,
readiness to serve others…
…qualities which are
within easy reach of every soul
are the foundations of one's
spiritual life…
Nelson Mandela

A Religious Martyr's Deep Thoughts Response
Commandments One and Two

The most important commandment is this:
The Lord our God is the only Lord.
Love the Lord your God with all your heart, with all
your soul, with all your mind,
and with all your strength.
The second most important commandment is this:
Love your neighbor as you love yourself.
Jesus of Nazareth

A Celebrated Ecologist's Deep Questions Response
War and Peace

*A primitive and deeply embedded human need
is inclusion within a tribal group.
Those within a tribe
protect and preserve their identity
from those outside their tribe, leading ultimately to
competition: violent and lethal, as in war,
and non-violent and non-lethal, as in peace.*
Edward O. Wilson

Religion,
the mitigating agency
between war and peace.
Leo Tolstoy

A Deep Thought…and an Answer
Why we are here…

We are here as one of those
who are seeking to find
through meditation
that spirit living within us…
telling us to listen to,
and follow
the wisdom in the humanities
and those religious teachings of prophets
in the parables and sermons
on love and search for peace within societies of mankind…
and for the love of our neighbor
given to
all who would hear.

An Ecumenical Hymn

Finlandia: This Is My Song

Music: Jon Sibelius
Lyrics: Eric Stone

This is my song, O God of all the nations
A song of peace for lands afar and mine
This is my home, the country where my heart is;
Here are my hopes, my dreams, my sacred shrine.
But other hearts in other lands are beating,
With hopes and dreams as true and high as mine.

My contry's skies are bluer than the ocean,
And sunlight beams on cloverleaf and pine.
But other lands have sunlight too and clover,
And skies are everywhere blue as mine.
O hear my song, O God of all the nations;
A song of peace for their land and for mine.

The Peace

The Peace
presents an opportunity for those gathered to
greet all of one's neighbors and reach out with
a handshake, a bow, a hug, or other appropriate
embrace, and with a cheerful,
encouraging verbal greeting
…and a smile.

The intent of the The Peace is to engage
the congregation
as a community of meditators and religious activists
rather than as individuals worshiping self-centeredly,
and to promote socialization amongst those gathered together.

A Humanist's Responsibility

...the opportunity for action may be fleeting.

Uniting Our Humanistic Beliefs with our Daily Actions

"The great end in life is not knowledge, but action."
Thomas H. Huxley

The great end in the expression of religious beliefs is neither concentration on the study and critiquing of sacred texts, the passive recitation of prayers, the rote performance of traditional liturgical exercises, nor a search for expiation of original or personal sin:
It is meaningful action.

The religious beliefs directed by the spirit dwelling deep within us will spring forth only as each one of us, each day, as members of the Earth's dominant species, translates these beliefs into selfless positive actions of agape love, the pragmatic expression of these beliefs.

The Humanist's Creed

To right those wrongs you have it within your power to change;

To practice actively the transcendent love
which enhances the welfare
of all sentient and non-sentient creatures;

To do unto others as you would have them do unto you;

To accept, protect, preserve, adapt to,
and learn to live in accord with
the limitations
of the thin biosphere
within which all life must co-exist.

Benediction

Benediction

Therefore, go forth with determination
to bring about change for the better
in human behavior—**yours**—one day at a time.
This day and each day, set a goal of compassion:

cheering the lost or lonely
charitable giving
visiting the sick, the depressed, the dying
consoling those griving
cheering the lost or lonely
or performing some act of environmental preservation
that you will achieve by the day's end.

And be of good spirit!
rejoicing in the beauty and blessings of Creation…
but being mindful always: *vita brevis, amore aeternitas…*
this life, this day, any day…could be the last that you will
ever have on Earth to bring about expression of your humanism.

Essential Reading

The Meaning of Human Existence
E.O. Wilson

The Social Conquest of Earth
E.O. Wilson

The Lessons of History
Will and Ariel Durant

The Varieties of Scientific Experience
Carl Sagan

The World Until Yesterday
Jared Diamond

Spirit and Nature: Why the Environment Is a Religious Issue
Stephen C. Rockefeller and John C. Elder (eds.)

Saving Jesus from the Church
Robin R. Meyers

About the Author

Robert William Christie
is a physician and medical scientist,
and a life-long Episcopalian who has served
as a Lay Reader, Eucharistic Minister,
and in many lay leadership capacities
in the several parishes to which he has belonged.
He has struggled over the years
to reconcile his head with his heart
in religious matters, and has belatedly realized
that he has become, in the wisdom of his later years,
an out of the closet Humanist
in need of an appropriate liturgy within which to frame
his values and beliefs, for himself and for other Humanists.

CPSIA information can be obtained at www.ICGtesting.com
Printed in the USA
BVOW11s1313090315

390742BV00001B/1/P